CROCUS

POETS
OUT LOUD
PRIZE
WINNERS

Jean Gallagher
This Minute, 2004

Lee Robinson
Hearsay, 2003

Janet Kaplan
The Glazier's Country, 2002

Robert Thomas
Door to Door, 2001

Julie Sheehan
Thaw, 2000

Jennifer Clarvoe
Invisible Tender, 1999

CROCUS

Karin Gottshall

Fordham University Press · New York · 2007

Copyright © 2007 Fordham University Press

All rights reserved. No part of this
publication may be reproduced,
stored in a retrieval system, or
transmitted in any form or by any
means—electronic, mechanical,
photocopy, recording, or any other
—except for brief quotations in
printed reviews, without the prior
permission of the publisher.

Library of Congress Cataloging-in-Publication Data

Gottshall, Karin.
Crocus / Karin Gottshall.—1st ed.
　p. cm.—(Poets out loud)
ISBN-13: 978-0-8232-2730-3 (cloth : alk. paper)
ISBN-13: 978-0-8232-2731-0 (pbk. : alk. paper)
ISBN-10: 0-8232-2730-8 (cloth : alk. paper)
ISBN-10: 0-8232-2731-6 (pbk. : alk. paper)
I. Title.
PS3607.O88C76　2007
811'.6—dc22
　　　　　　　　　　　　　　　2007000872

Printed in the United States of America
09　08　07　5　4　3　2
First edition

For my parents, and for Terry

Contents

I

The Exile's Tale 3
Threshold 5
Echo 7
The Ghost 8
The Lure of the Exotic 9
The Raspberry Room 10
Our Lady of the Briars 11
The Otter 12
I was in bed all day with the sun 13
Insomnia 14
Inheritance 15
Keeping House 16
The Older Man 18
The Talaria 19
Pot Washing at Le Lapin d'Or 21
A Fable 22

II

The Revenant 25
The Bog Body 26
Mallards 28
Whether 29
Roanoke 31
The Riddle 32

Through and Through Me 34
Cold Front 35
Unborn 36
Summer 37
The Stone 38
Tender 40
The Ministry of Snow 41
The Ashes 42
A Walking Tour 43
The Lost World 44

III

The Current 49
The Alice Experiment 51
Blizzard 57
Let's hold it again to the light 59
The Creation of Rain 60
Despite Myself 61
Unreliable Clock 63
The Grassland 64
At the Window 66
Describing the Bliss 67

Acknowledgments

Grateful acknowledgment is made to the editors of the following journals, in which versions of these poems first appeared:

Black Warrior Review: "The Raspberry Room."
Cairn: "The Lure of the Exotic"; "Unreliable Clock."
Connecticut Review: "The Grassland."
The Gettysburg Review: "The Alice Experiment."
Green Mountains Review: "Describing the Bliss"; "Roanoke."
Greensboro Review: "Mallards."
Hunger Mountain: "The Otter."
Louisville Review: "The Lost World."
Mid-American Review: "The Ghost"; "Pot Washing at Le Lapin d'Or."
New England Review: "The Revenant"; "Whether."
North American Review: "The Current."
Poet Lore: "The Ministry of Snow."
The Red Wheelbarrow: "Blizzard."
Shenandoah: "Insomnia."
The Southern Review: "At the Window"; "Threshold"; "Our Lady of the Briars."
Spoon River Poetry Review: "A Fable."
Tar River Poetry: "The Ashes"; "Inheritance."
Two Rivers Review: "Keeping House"; "Let's hold it again to the light."
Virginia Quarterly Review: "The Exile's Tale."

"The Ashes" was reprinted in Ted Kooser's weekly newspaper column, "American Life in Poetry."

Thanks to Alberto Ríos, Elisabeth Frost, Helen Tartar, and to the many friends and teachers who have been indispensable in the creation of this book.

Special thanks to Mary Ruefle, Clare Rossini, Jody Gladding, Gary Margolis, Ruth Stone, Stephanie Painter, members of the Spring Street Poets, Kate Schmitt, and Ted at the Middlebury P.O.

Extra special thanks to Mark Cox: my teacher always.

I

The Exile's Tale

The country I come from is far to the north:
our wedding dresses are lined with wolf's fur and the stars
are fixed. We share the dwellings of white bears,
who never wake from their winter sleep,

whose dreams, in the religion of my land, comprise
the human soul. In my country the snow
lies as deep as four men are tall, and the fish
below the ice are the color of meteor-streaks—

it's said they embody a timeless grief. That place
lies so far north that natural laws are sometimes reversed,
and careless girls have been known to be released
from gravity, to float away and be lost forever

among the waiting constellations. We call this
The Union of Here and There, and though
it brings sorrow to the mothers, the event is a lucky omen,
and is celebrated with a feast lasting one hundred days.

The great art of my land is inscribed on ice; its epics
are recited from the face of the deckle-edged moon.
The sun appears for just one minute of one day
each year—only the merest skin of it breaks

over the surface of our horizon, and the occasion
is pointedly ignored. My land is so far to the north

that our radios pick up nothing but strange, ancient operas broadcast from the Pleiades, and our language

has no term for *cold*. For how can you name that which is all you've ever known, the substance from which your words are cut, in which your shadow resides and your breath goes wandering—that of which you are built entirely?

Threshold

Awake at dawn, I'm looking out
at a perfect row of tiny handprints
coming up the walk, pressed

into the dusting of new snow.
In the pale light I'm still shaking off
last night's dream, and as I've hoped

for a child I am willing, now, to believe
that during the night one walked on her hands
from somewhere beyond

the woodpile, straight to my front door.
I open it now. There's no sign of her.
In the grainy spring snow the tracks

are etched precisely: five slim fingers,
each tipped with a dash for a claw. Dear angel
of wildness, it's not what I thought,

this evidence of arrival, though I know
you're fierce and soft and brave.
The conventions of breakfast await,

and the sun has already reached the pavement
where your first tracks are lost
against gray stone. Into the yard I throw

an apple, a corncob, a handful
of raisins. The landlord wouldn't
approve of your boldness, or this reward

for the straight, fading path of your paws—
the way you came right to the threshold
as if to astonish or entreat me.

Echo

Now you're bird or sting-fish
on the monitor, all shockwave and light.
Heart, I've called you heavy, I've called you
troubled and hard—oh,

broken. Heart of rain, heart of crushing
weight and ruin, you bear all the steely
reckonings of my history,
mistaken and perilous. I thought

you'd grown weak, alone so long
in an unlit cavern. How could I
know your deep electric tunings,
or the delicacy of your gills? Now I see

you're pure and whole as star-shine. I hear
your furious strength. Hard-wired,
by necessity, you sing
to and through me the dark

and difficult passages of the song's
complexity—revealed
and clear-voiced, the purpled timbre
of your music.

The Ghost

How many times have I met her (a small,
reasoning thing)—her face in the frost
on the window or shrouded by birdsong

in a winter tree where cardinals flicker
like lamps in the wind? How many times have I
met her on dusty roads where katydids fret

in the catnip and vetch and the full moon drifts
like an anchor in the blue sky? This is my ghost's
sorrow: she says she would comfort me,

show me her wounds. She says the darkness
is a soft bed. *But the soul. . . .* I say,
and she smiles. *How to explain to you*

the nature of the soul. . . . Think of a spoon,
she says, *an object for the most part utilitarian,*
though lovely, your initials engraved on the handle.

Who has given you this gift? On what occasion?
For what have you used it? Most important—and let's
say, for the sake of argument, that darkness

is all that endures—endures beyond this brief
banquet at which we both partake—where then
would you place such an object, to keep it safe?

The Lure of the Exotic

In the archipelago they tell of a boy
who grew up in a tree—what is there
to do in a tree, with only the companionship
of the wind? He read each leaf,

line by line. He handled the surface
of his every thought like a sharp-cut gem.
It was almost visible—the crown
he'd fashioned of them, where it rested

on his brow. And, it's said, in the right
conditions you could see all the way
through him—the wandering arteries,
the sails of his lungs filling

and emptying. On the horizon the mist
fell and lifted and fell over the currents, sliced
by the fin of some creature out of legend.
You can't *live* like that, the islanders

cried, the childless women, like knots,
loosening at the sight of him. They were right—
he'd disappeared by the following year.
They wondered was it worth it: that adventure

of balance in four wide dimensions, the moonlight
pouring through him, for the strange end
he'd come to when he stepped down
toward the cool white-veined blue of the sky.

The Raspberry Room

It was solid hedge, loops of bramble and thorny
as it had to be with its berries thick as bumblebees.
It drew blood just to get there, but I was queen
of that place, at ten, though the berries shook like fists
in the wind, daring anyone to come in. I was trying
so hard to love *this* world—real rooms too big and full
of worry to comfortably inhabit—but believing I was born
to live in that cloistered green bower: the raspberry patch
in the back acre of my grandparents' orchard. I was cross-
stitched and beaded by its fat, dollmaker's needles. The effort
of sliding under the heavy, spiked tangles that tore
my clothes and smeared me with juice was rewarded
with space, wholly mine, a kind of room out of
the crush of the bushes with a canopy of raspberry
dagger-leaves and a syrup of sun and birdsong.
Hours would pass in the loud buzz of it, blood
made it mine—the adventure of that red sting singing
down my calves, the place the scratches brought me to:
just space enough for a girl to lie down.

Our Lady of the Briars

At dusk a doe walks the broken-
tiled hallway, skitters out across
the kitchen garden's still-defined plot
overwrought with chicory and wild

carrot. A shadow makes her flinch and bolt,
while below the hill the far-flung Hudson carves
its agenda into stone, grinds heavily on—to Bear
Mountain, then Manhattan. The bats

are soft charcoal against the sky's palette
of blue and silver and pink. Fruit
still scents the rambling orchard, its antique
pears and apples small and sour now,

for the animals alone. Grapevines
dismantle the brick dormitory; it will take
another hundred years to level, though the cloister's
fallen to ruin already, its rubble

a complicated mosaic around the crumbled
fountain. Its roof put off like a wimple.
The hushed interior, burnished and storied,
is held like a face to the darkening, creatured air.

The Otter

In dreams you're like the otter I saw
under the bridge one day—where the river is lined
with shadow-dappled boulders, trees
drawn up from the bank as if in alarm—or rather,
you look at me like she did, and I'm looking back
with the same surprise and sorrow (because I knew
she would soon slip into the water and away); she looked
at me for just a few heartbeats—not fear, it seemed, between us,
so much as recognition, a memory—looked at me
as you do in dreams: our brown eyes caught
for a moment between softness and a kind
of helpless, inevitable forgetting; and then I haven't
seen you move, I don't hear a splash, but where you were
there is no one, and the rest of the dream is me
trying to voice something meaningless but of absolute
importance (the way, walking back along the gravel track
I chanted *water, otter, water, otter,* until the chant became
a plea or prayer), trying to remember how I arrived at the spot
where you were, and when I realized you were gone.

I was in bed all day with the sun

and a heavy dictionary.
I watched the cat fall asleep
on the woven rug. Outside

a bird unspooled its song in wide,
round loops: drifting off,
coming back. Memory is like that—

words loosed like dust motes,
a dream I slip into: this cat's
green-eyed mother, her grave

under licorice root and money trees.
Then come the angels of the afternoon
with their wings of flame.

One day language will unbind itself
from me—even to the barest
particulars: the first time

I heard the word *crocus*, the new
spring sun on my shoulder, smell
of mud—quick freshet
working itself free. At last
to release this word *I*
into the long blue currents of the sea.

Insomnia

You say, *Come, loosen my thoughts*
like a braid undone. You say, *Give me again*
my secret name. Listen: the apples of wet snow
are falling from the moonlit branches.
You count them, soggy windfall, call them
Hour Hand and Sour Dawn. Heart
is beating the night song to the prickle
of starlight, but there's a racket, far off:
soldiers, perhaps, pitching their tents
on the bank of the Canadian lake—
the one where your grandmother warned you
to be quiet; smooth water carries voices
so clearly to the far shore. Once a girl wept all night
at its sandy strand, and the villagers opposite
dreamed of their first sorrows. You say,
Come, soothe her with your warm hands,
slip the pine needles from her hair. The foxes
are hunting under the willow again—yes,
they're restless, too, they have her hungry eyes—
their strong red bodies shift bright
as morning's banner lifted against the sky.

Inheritance

During the snowiest winter on record
my grandpa found that old dresser
in the woods, in a snow bank, under a white

pine where a blue jay perched cursing
all day into his kazoo. It was so cold
the snow slid from the wood like layers of thin

cloth. Good cherry, the drawers still pulled
smooth, stashed with a squirrel's full
dowry of acorns. It was carted home

where Grandpa stripped it, stained
it, stenciled a wild iris on top. All the years
of my growing up the dresser held

strange treasure: rubber bands, antique
hardtack, a daguerreotype of the moon. I knew
one day it would belong to me, like the familial

bad temper, bad back, and unceasing love
of the difficult. All its heavy burden
would be mine. *Fine old dresser*, Grandpa

would say, *big, sturdy, that someone left out
in the snow.* Hands spread, he said: *so sturdy you
could hitch a horse to it, ride it around the world.*

Keeping House

For seven years my mother stood
before a row of wood panels,
lacquered shiny black, creating
a Chinese palace scene with oil paint
and gold leaf. I used to watch her work,
the careful way she stepped back sometimes,
her brush in her mouth, to better see

the place where the chrysanthemums
would go in neat rows, the necessary
gesture of the boy carrying buckets
of water. It was an inspiration, to make
that screen, and most of my childhood
was spent in its rich presence, its courtiers
in their silk gowns of rose and green

prominent in my dreams. How beautiful
they were, how orderly their rooms
and courtyards. Meanwhile dirty plates
filled the sink, clothes overflowed
the hamper, the crack in the kitchen
window was never fixed,
the garden went unweeded

and finally all to seed.
Still my mother calmly painted
the flute player entertaining the nobles,
the distant mountains. I always expected

to be like her: to make my balance
between the grubby leavings
of the rummage-sale world

and the clean work of the heart. We used
to laugh hard at the table cluttered
with records and socks. I wonder
which of those figures has become my godmother:
the woman combing her hair on a blue cushion,
maybe, or the one looking out at the horizon,
folding her fan. It must have been from them

I learned the sweetness of a cupboard of clean
bowls, to love folding the clothes
while the wind blows snow
against the windows. But it's because of my mother
that I know why it's called *keeping* house
—that the art of housework
is also in knowing what *never*

to clean: the line of footprints in cerulean
the cat described from the studio to the kitchen
after he walked across her palette;
those small, shimmering ovals my fingertips left
on the banister after I found
the balsawood box holding the thin,
breath-blown sheets of gold leaf.

The Older Man

White-on-white like tumbled
sheets, the crumpled paper. It was autumn;
I spent hours sketching the dancers
in the Degas galleries. Five times
a day I heard the docent say Degas portrayed
his dancers, his bathers like unthinking
animals—but I was in love
with their arched backs, the blatant pleasures
and fidgets of the body in use. Your apartment,
dim and small, was in a neighborhood redolent
of cinnamon. I was clunky in corduroy
and wool as you tenderly unwound
my scarf each night; it seemed your cat
would never leave off worshipping
my ankles. You unbuttoned
my heavy coat, received my load of books,
and set before me, once, a baked pear—rich
with brown sugar, sweet
butter, redundant with spice. I ate it
ravenously, that exotic food.

The Talaria

Lovelorn, I'm sketching the ancient marbles
at the Met when I find that I am capable,
at least in part, of flight—rising up from myself

and over the bronze armor, glass cases, girls
in Catholic school uniforms stroking the stone
calves of Apollo, thinking they're out

of the guard's sight. I am floating
high above the grave stele of a child kissing
her doves goodbye—a twenty-five-hundred-year

farewell—and through the columns of daylight
slanting in from Fifth Avenue, toward the delicate,
repetitive sculptures of egg-and-dart,

surprised that this domed expanse of limestone
is broad enough to hold me. The students giggle
behind their hands and there is an amplitude

in the great hall's echoing—its spaciousness—
vast enough to inhabit. And that small scrap
of blue below, still holding her pencil, is me.

I am considering Io: transformed
by Zeus into a white cow, she scratched her name
in the sand with a dainty hoof so her father

would know her. What announcement
can I make to my earth-bound body, skeptical
of metamorphosis? I must think of the trick,

fix the message to the white page—convince
the figure ballasted by sadness that joy is a vaulted
chamber: wide to rise into, musical with whispers.

Pot Washing at Le Lapin d'Or

Not my first job, but the first time
I felt the sweat from my hairline
pool at my collarbone, felt my shoulders

harden to bandy muscle.
I'd spent my junior year studying French,
but all that summer my right arm practiced

its broad, native O, circling the rims
of the tremendous, battered stock pots,
fry pans, strainers, and double boilers.

First time I felt the steely pride
of doing the work no one wanted—
and first time, in all the slop and soreness

of the body's effort I felt beautiful: in cutoffs
and stained apron, steam curling the wisps
from my braid, flushing my arms

while I scoured the aluminum salad bowl
so big I could have curled myself
into it like the hare in the moon—

but instead set it shining on the drying rack,
its silver mouth wide, as if surprised
by our mutual accomplishment.

A Fable

There was a girl who set out with a tiger
on a long journey. She'd never before left her home

but he came to her with his startled eyes
and she left the dishes drying on the wooden rack,

the linens folded in the closet, left her flowered
dresses and the complicated song of fear

to travel with him among rocks, in meadows of wild iris.
They walked through the deep pastures and slept

in the wind, on soft grasses. They walked
and walked, and in the end that's all they had—

they weren't magical beings, they couldn't know
each others' hearts. Through the loops and arteries

of their clean bodies slid their secret sorrows,
and in no place in this world could they lay them down—

they loved the sight too much: the snow
and clear streams, the leaping birds.

The Revenant

The shore road hems a thousand, thousand
acres of orchards, honey stands and curio shops
quaint as cross-stitch, and curves past the house

where my grandmother was born—its tumble
of roses, sturdy square columns, shattered dormers.
At the headland, Lake Ontario mulls its secrets:

the millennial grit-minerals cast up as smooth
black stones. Steel gray, the breakers. A resident ghost
haunts the lighthouse grounds, a widow forever

regarding her inheritance of loss—the shifting waters—
a myth built on phosphoric night-sightings and sobbing
winds, the tired, insistent percussion

of this promontory. I will admit I believe in her: a spirit
culled from the interplay of human grief and weather.
Standing dizzy and shivering at the pierhead's tip

I won't say this place remembers me, nor
that I've been here before, even in dreams.
But I know the specter's ancestral lace, this ornate

veiling of freshwater foam; I understand her dormancies
and nocturnal visitations. I recognize the pitch
and plungings—the keening treble of her cry.

The Bog Body

Cherry-tinted slurry, freshwater snails, mother-
of-pearl—for my first kiss I was hip-deep
in a slow-running river laced with tannic acid; I took in

the river's lesson of concealment. I thought
of the woman from the Danish bog, whose taut remains
stretched across a page of my ecology text,

an Iron Age sacrifice given over to the preserving gods
of reed and peat. Did I even know I had a body
before that kiss broke its boundaries? How vulnerable

we are to passion, to the mud-body's aspirations
toward some notion of eternity. And the fens
and sphagnum bogs in collusion, keeping their secrets

like mouthed coins. Afterwards I felt heavy,
a mail-coat on my skin as if I'd taken up
that steel-shot river to wear. Another day

our teacher took us far into the wetlands
and we walked a mile or so, tentative,
on spongy moss, and then he had us wade a stream—

only an inch deep, he teased, and so it looked,
but we sank into the bog's kiss of sediment muck.
Laboring in that thick, gritty element I came eye-to-eye

with a squirrel's skull, blasted hollow, clean white
and spirit-like, resting on the porous ground.
I lifted it, expecting to find the whole structure

of ribs and spinal column, pelvis and leg-bones
intact, but it was just that floating head,
a miniature Yorick's comic grin. Watery places

were mystical to the ancients—my vision
was of myself as mineral puzzle. The bog
promised a lightless but durable afterlife.

My death began when pleasure announced itself
and burdened me with weight: ambitions
built on bone and breath—so tenuously preserved.

Mallards

The river in our town ran brown as dark coffee,
but nothing could keep me from its water
when I snuck through the scrub brush, shattered
glass and burdock to wade. Same as the ducks, I was
unmindful of muck water, foam cups in their slime coats
cached in the space between tree roots, concrete slabs
upended and sprouting ridged steel rods like feelers.
I thought they were "my lords"; costumed bridegrooms,
that flash of emerald, shiver of green and metallic
shimmer. Princely though common—the townies
called them beggars, trash birds, threw them junk
food. To me they embodied *handsome*—that crisp
neck band a noble distinction. Their noise: raucous
with rage-calls and mating, clamor, and contagion.
I was nine and thought myself queenly, ankle-deep
in the chemical runoff, the suck water draining
off the agricollege, a ring of those suitors around me
for my stale crumbs. It was the heartland—
everything big—the sky phosphoric blue, the bridges
arching their backs high over the sluiceway,
the slurry, the unclaimed river of what nobody wanted.

Whether

Aligned with the mechanism
whereby the spirit is borne aloft
through song comes again

the question: whether. And not soothed
so much as opened by the boy
soprano's *Sanctus*, what moves

in the mind as the throat constricts
in sympathy, one note peeled
from the last, fine as paper slipped

from a garlic bulb, veined,
translucent, is *whether*—as if
wound through the spiraling

amplitude, purpled, fretted,
one voice suspended
in concentration of prayer or terror

wills itself above faltering,
more perfect since time must
soon break it. And made it.

Whether and by whatever impossible
arrangement of stars, harmonies,
correspondences through which

the music finds the spirit and like
a blade slits and releases,
circulates the question

through the phrase, the delicate
engine—as if it matters: the song
rises, everything goes with it.

Roanoke

Where did I start, to end here—
this grave of moss and brown beetles,
my English rose strewn across the curved
Atlantic? The ark I had built inside my body
turned out with the tide
and the sweet voice of Raleigh,
a whisper from the far coast.

I was not seduced. I sought
a harbor more brackish,
a blacker berry, something to stain
the hands with sacrifice.
I tell you: all dreams begin with leaving,
and death is the only arrival.
It's the island barely visible, stretching itself
like a fog over the pines of America,
the shadows of its birds passing slowly over our skins.

My mother's garden
is blooming across the sea. Tiny sloops
line the channel, the fishermen
haul in their loaded nets. The black mud
of Virginia will take me apart, mineral
by mineral; what is left is the hard
journey of our skeletons, the emptied dish
of my eye pressed firmly to the ground.

The Riddle

The answer is not an egg, though egg-like
it has no door. She imagines a church
from the outside—the windows' stories seamed

with lead—or the little chapel she used to make
with her fingers. She guesses speckled shell,
silk lining, a vaulted white hall. Thinks of eggs

gathered in a wire basket—though basket is closer,
or even wire. A containing vacancy, like the holes
in the wire weave, something like a weir—

perhaps a net? She's been searching so long,
the snow falling, each flake lathed and polished;
she has been primed for precision by ice

and hunger. She thinks of the spaces
between the flakes, and then of the spaces
in the flakes themselves—like thresholds

for only the tiniest notion to pass through.
Surely there is gold. So like an egg. . . .
And there can be no question it's smooth—

she thinks of brushing lightly the honey-hued
glass, stroking the glowing robes and crowns,
the empty, distorting ovals: bubbles

in the cooled and sanctified glaze. Inside
the secret shines, coalescing in ceremony,
armored, entire and still. Like an egg: waiting.

Through and Through Me

Slender—my means that cold
November when, coming home to Brooklyn
late from my job, the wind off the bay
clapped my hands. And tender—almost—
my recollection of that slight young woman,
baking a yam to share with the gray cat.
But it trips me up every time—memory—
to think she was *me*, and mesmerizing:
that scene of who I was, refracted down
through forgotten days. The dry, early snow slants
perpetually at the glass of those broad
windows. As it darkens the lamplight shows
the room reflected in them, and the snow
seems to be falling in that other room which
is also full of the ghosts of trees, the lit
candles of other kitchens. The room warms
as the radiators bang and the cat waits,
shifting on his chair. She seems almost
graceful, the memory-creature.
She sets down the plates and eats,
her image in collage with the cat, the trees,
the snow—glazed in light against black windows.

Cold Front

Last night
the weather shifted;
the winds
swept the compass
and the body responded,

like the billowing
sheers—the loose weave
of the capillaries
filling and released.
When the gale
entered the tree
the leaves took it
entirely, nothing

was held back or denied;
the body turned
on its bed,
sobbing, saying,
Life, why won't you hold me . . .

Unborn

I've seen the shape
    of your longing
by the stone wall,
    popping with nimble

fingers the packed seedpods
    of jewelweed. Again
in the maple, sailing
    the wind in that tall-masted

vessel. You seek
    my heat and untried body's
guesswork; you could
    come forth from me complete.

At night I lay myself down
    smooth as water, but I have
astonishing dreams:
    you paint scene after scene

of your desire—my long,
    empty arms—
and waking I see you
    in the frightened animals

crossing the road, hear you
    in the rising insistence
of the cicada—small
    sailor of the wheat field,

sailor of air.

Summer

Overwrought and scented—the woods blare
like a big pipe organ. Impractical song
and sun—flamboyant poppies and irises peopling
the fragrant garden. Impractical indigo
bunting, flitting on the branch of the scrabbly pine
like a piece of bright jewelry. Yes, there is a home
underground—dark enough and we'll indeed
lie down with the bones of little foxes
and it will seep through like black ink
on a butterfly's wing. How conservative, the breaking
down, the loaming and weaving together of the buried—
how ornate, the resurrection! Does
the firm ground appear like heaven, then, to what
emerges? The shiny bugs are walking the stalks
as if they were the fabled byways; the long day
spins out in reckless radiance.

The Stone

Central Park in autumn, a festival with tents
and merchants' booths—I walk the wet, curving pavements
to find the psychic's, cross his palm

with silver. He cups my fingers and closes them
around a milky stone he says will give me flight—it's cold
but his skin is soft, he holds my hand and his warmth

travels—his touch a new heat through me. Already, though,
I've gasped and begun to rise. I feel myself
lifting from my body like a glove peeled off. Fog

snakes below me through the park; the city's misty exhalation
recedes with the glint of the ring sellers' stalls. I search
the miniature crowds for my abandoned form as the bare wind

whips around the banners, the vapor-ribbons of white,
and I gain altitude over the parti-colored tents, the reservoir,
distant skyscrapers I always feared to mount,

the Hudson like a long jade arm—all seen through frayed rags
of the clouds' understory. I've longed for this: solitude, remove,
but the air chills and I'm breathless and distracted—

that contact before separation, the seer's hand on mine, the heat
and intimacy, his granite eyes. What's more, I'm worried
for my body, sweatered and childlike, left propped

among the swirling leaves on a wire chair. My descent
is like a wish withdrawn; the wind an orchestra
tuning—I drop through the trees, see the psychic still bent

over my hand as I approach my rigid body and press
against my own blood-filled chest. I dissolve and am restored
to flesh. One moment more of the clairvoyant's clasp

and I'm released—he's moved on to the next seeker
and I'm left with only the heat of my own biology
for comfort, the long gray scarf around my neck.

Tender

In his shyness my grandfather, awkward
at child-talk, sent me searching each Sunday for treasure
among the jewel-bright jars of quince jelly,
stacks of rim-chipped saucers, and the giant coins

of pie tins in his kitchen cupboards. By means
of animal crackers, coloring books, and candy bracelets
his love was silently and incrementally revealed, and I
became so cunning at the hunt that the hiding places

had to be shifted and rethought: a finger puppet
cradled in an egg cup, fruit leather between the pages
of my grandmother's cookbook. Once I found
a child's ceramic tea set, Blue Willow, nestled

in the napkin drawer, a richness beyond dreaming.
In my five-year-old heart I cringed at the fragility—hoped
only to get it home before I broke it. But under the sugar
bowl's lid was something more: a two-dollar bill,

folded small as a fingertip. The fleur-de-lis of its green
within the vanilla-white of cheap porcelain, the billowing
boughs of Chinese trees, doves kissing mid-air,
was my first cash—it smelled of apples from his orchard

and the cracking leather of his wallet. Money-hungry,
I thought of blackbirds in singing flight from an opened pie—
but it was not to be spoken of, the secret currency
of a reclusive nation: his trust declared, unspendable.

The Ministry of Snow

The snow having begun, you know
it will fall all night, stroking
the house so softly you will

accept the ministry
of animals: the deep heart
beats and dreams of cats asleep

beside you. In the kitchen
the stack of plates, composed
in the dark cupboard, winks

with a rim of gold. It's the watchfulness
of grandmothers, that glimmer.
Loneliness is the price you pay

for loving the snow, just now, more
than you love the chatter and crises
of your hungry life. Loneliness

curls around the house like the settling
of noiseless snow; believe
in the counsel of drifting, of cold.

The Ashes

You were carried here by hands
and now the wind has you: gritty
as incense, dark sparkles borne

in the shape of blowing,
this great atmospheric bloom
spinning under the bridge and expanding—

shape of wind and its pattern
of shattering. Having sloughed off
the urn's temporary shape,

there is another of you now—
tell me which to speak to:
the one you were, or are, the one who waited

in the ashes for this scattering, or the one
now added to the already haunted woods,
the woods that sigh and shift their leaves—

where your mystery billows, then breathes.

A Walking Tour

The horse barn's been knocked down; the cottage
I rented on Painted Turtle Pond for two years is abandoned,
a haven this August day for damselflies, the shrill mosquito.

I used to walk here, my boots crunching through rime frost
in October, the far-wandering village dogs so gentle they must
have grown up reading Dickens. The landlady

filled the old manor with antiques, tiles
from France painted with birds so lovely my eyes
stung; she made honey and goat's

cheese, but the house is empty now. For how
long? In the graveyard the crickets assert themselves; it's time
someone set the stones right, though they're worn

smooth, illegible. Shaker Hill Road
was almost impassable by December, its haunted houses
entrusted to their caretaker-ghosts and the quiet,

resourceful deer. Difficult even by late November—the path
to the creek—but the Catskills
were laid out on the horizon like the folded hands

of a kind grandfather, and the horse farm was covered
with white, where the horses *lived*—paced
their long and weather-rich days on the sloping acres.

The Lost World

The state-of-the-art animatronic T-Rex
hits the harbor like a typhoon,
takes out warehouse walls,
city buses, bites a man in half

like I would eat a Vlasic pickle. Later,
in grainy black and white, my recurring dream
of apocalypse: dark, heavy snow falls for days
and when it melts the ground

goes right ahead and melts, too, and there is not
an island, not a speck
of land for refuge—and then
we all go down. She went down, once,

the small girl I was, to the rim of the hot
tide beside the sea's countless gas-
lit ballrooms. The Aztecs believed butterflies
were the returned spirits of warriors

killed in battle; if I could
believe it, if I could believe anything
so much as *remains*. How do I break
it to the small girl, still ankle-wet

at the edge, that the sun, the sea itself
is not beyond extinction, the resources
of her skinny body stacked inside her?
Shall I say goodbye

now? Because it's lost for good:
the feast of flowers,
brontosaurs moving like ships
through the morning mist. Not to mention

my beginning: those days before I knew how much,
how keenly, I could miss.

The Current

Lake Superior wash me smooth
as the frosted lozenge of beach glass
I found on the sandspit—worry bead,

charm for luck, bearing the letter A
in low relief. Wash me clean
as that origin, whole as the note

rising from the Russian freighter,
the wind's long vowel.
Scour me with your ice waves.

As a girl I learned your metals
by heart: copper from Isle Royale, iron ore
staining the harbor red. I studied your giant

wolf's head and chanted the puzzle words
of Keweenaw, Ishpeming, Sault St. Marie.
I was raised on cold cash and water

heavy with minerals; our tap
crusted green and faceted as a geode.
I grew with a weird blood-hunger

for stone-food, déjà vu among horses,
and the need, irresistible, to enter
perilous currents. Accept my return.

City on the hill, smokestacks
of Duluth, bear witness—water wear
me back to my beginning.

The Alice Experiment

Alice Liddell, seven, is costumed
as "The Beggar Maid," posed
in the Deanery garden's mossy corner
at Christ Church, rags slipping

from her slim shoulder, eyes fixing
the camera assuredly. Her right hand's
cupped, not quite in supplication, close
to her waist. The left's balled,

a tight fist at her hip. Facing page: Alice
in her best gown, same wall, its ivy
a living frame for the girl in her flounced
and spotted dress, head tilted down—demurely,

you might think, except her eyes,
in soft focus, regard the photographer
with a certain shrewdness. She's Carroll's favorite
model—she knows what she looks like.

   *

At seven I jumped with the neighbor girl
on her parents' bed. We chanted

My Name is Alice and *Six Drunken Sailors*
wearing fringed skirts and flip-flops, the tiny mirrors

on my halter top throwing shimmers
across the textured ceiling. The forbidden

patch of trees out back was *The Forest*—thick
with used condoms and beer cans, evidence

and artifacts. The sprawling apartment complex
where we lived we called *The Castle*.

One day we happened on the hatch
of its winding crawlspace—the labyrinth

below the brick buildings which we claimed
as ours, bringing pilfered flashlights and sugar

cigarettes. Once we knew of it, how could we not want
to travel in the underground spaces

where the super had to stoop and grunt but we
could run quick as rabbits among the pipes and wiring?

I remember the crypt-smell of earth, the cobwebs
like ghost fingers against my cheeks. I remember

being hauled up by the collar, spitting curses.

*

Of course we never
adventured alone:
there were stray cats
who followed for bits

of meat or kindness,
and our imaginary friends,
half-animal too.
We could see them,

trailing us in the dim light,
royal and bejeweled,
but murderous pirates
nonetheless—blades

between their teeth.
And once I found
the skeleton of a mouse,
paper-white and curled

as if in sleep, delicate.
Its spirit, I feared, slipped,
on little mouse feet, into
the dark hollow of my ear.

   *

Julia Margaret Cameron photographed
her child-subjects as tousle-haired cherubs, angels
of the Annunciation, in nativity scenes,
allegories: "Goodness" and "Grief." She posed
Alice, twenty and ever the Greek scholar's daughter,
as Ceres. The young woman stares intensely
from a shower of greenery; she's long since
fallen out with Carroll. In another picture
she's Agnes, patron saint of girls,
who, at 13, was ridiculed for her faith
and made to strip in a brothel. Accounts vary
on the manner of her death—she may
have been burnt at the stake, beheaded,
or stabbed through the throat. On her feast day,
the folk wisdom goes, *say a Paternoster, stick a pin
in your sleeve and you will dream of the one you will marry.*

			*

My mother said if I tried very hard
I might remember my previous life,
having so recently left it. It was easier
to recall what had come between;
when I closed my eyes I could still hear
the pulsing hum of the Bardo,
where I'd seen the possibilities, and chosen.
I was taken to Disney's "Alice."
Afterward I dreamed in cartoon—I liked
to be solid like that, to have no
inside. The neighbor girl had a jack-in-the-box
from which the Caterpillar popped with his hookah,
asking the question *"Who are you?"*
I had a doll of the Cheshire Cat—his teeth
glowed in the dark. In my dreams
I heard his gravelly voice, between a growl
and a purr, whispering *"we're all mad here . . ."*

			*

The neighbors I remember: the girl of course,
and her mother, a sculptor of marble. Piece by piece

her women emerged from stone. There was the cop
who showed me his gun, which I coveted

until I learned he'd tried to shoot
the stray cat Dad rescued for our pet. Pregnant

and not yet full-grown she'd wandered the hallways,
howling for food and love. College kids

offered me sips of beer and tokes of weed—I felt
welcome anywhere I didn't get thrown out of.

The white-haired lady who saw me by the swimming
pool pretending to be Dorothy, dragging a stuffed dog

on a piece of yarn, thought I was someone else—
"Mary Ann, Mary Ann," she kept calling, "get over here,

Mary Ann." And there was the guy downstairs
who gave out spider rings at Halloween and took

my photograph as Peter Pan next to his color TV. The picture
scared me—my eyes sparked red malice in the flash.

   *

Xie Kitchin stands erect in the page's costume—Viola
disguised as Cesario—her hand at her waist,
mouth and eyes set, serious. Who told her
that's the look a boy wears? In "Penitence"
Carroll has cornered her like Alice in the garden,
her nightgown trailing and her fingers laced, not quite in
 prayer.
It wasn't unusual for Victorian children to be photographed
kissing chastely, but Cameron pressed her tiny subjects
 together,
open mouthed, and titled the albumen print "Turtle Doves."
Of her peculiar gaze and focus she said, *when I saw
something that to my eye was very beautiful I stopped there.*
Carroll himself recalled that he sent Alice straight off
down the rabbit hole, *without the least idea
what was to happen afterwards.*

   *

I had a Red Riding Hood doll whose skirt
could be flipped to get the grandmother;
pull Granny's bonnet over her face

and the wolf appeared. There's no comfort
or repose in a thing so violently divided,
but it exerts a kind of reckless magic.

Hadn't the neighbor girl said she could see my heart
through the skin of my chest? Hadn't I grown a foot
and didn't my body ache with a life so forceful

it was practically immortality? I had
long rambles underground with the cat,
whose habit was to lure me deep

into the tunnels, then wink and disappear.
All the spirits of small things drew near,
whispering their dry, insistent warnings,

but I was Defiance herself—going all the way in.

Blizzard

This is the snow you've read about in stories,
where the magic bear emerges from the wood
to carry the girl on his broad back. Gossamer,

you might call the blizzard, hung in air like a rack
of gowns, only gossamer means "goose of summer,"
and this is midwinter and the only thing stitching

its way through these clouds-come-to-ground is a trio
of crows—the wind pushing them higher
than their course. Tulle, then, in bolts and bolts, veils

in tight arrangement upon the crocuses
that needled up during last week's thaw,
against the foreheads of the peaked Victorians

across the street; think of the dresses they wore,
stiff white satin tight at the bodice,
the circle of pearls—the trees wear that now.

Better to be indoors, where it just glazes
the window-glass, and simply imagine the slow
embroidery of lace and beadwork across the lake's

breast. Nothing tames a person more completely
than magic—isn't that what the folktales
teach? Watch, then: the stubborn birds

are dressing themselves in the light, cold fabric
of the storm and the bear rambles the city,
white as this draped shawl of whitest snow.

Let's hold it again to the light:

the memory of the glow and fire
of the glassblower's studio
where we stood during the full scumble
of a winter storm, watched him gather
the molten glass to the blowpipe
and work it while the heat of that furnace
flushed our faces, so happy
in our new love. Since memory's heavy
detritus is so much slush and slag, the old
unfulfilled joys we wake
clutching after, let's claim it completely—
the vase we watched formed
from the dry, hot air and red,
as later you traced the line from wrist
to shoulder to crown, chasing that
heat and contact, held and gathered,
saying yes—we can make something finally
out of emptiness and breath.

The Creation of Rain

There is something in rain that drives me
to weep as well. One could
say the weather is a woman, combing
long hair, or weather is the trying on
of fabrics: silks and velvet, rough wool,
today's thick canvas. All one long winter

I watched from my window: the same
street, grubby houses, the same man
on a bike towing a shopping cart full
of heavy parts—gears and pulleys—
that daily rattling. Under the flyaway
sky his scraps could have been the props

of weather: levers to hitch the cloud-
cover, tip the sleet's canisters. There is that
in weeping which cannot help but make
us think of weather. Shadows
of clouds against the mountain's brow,
those grays and umbers and under

the colors the making of color,
the light of this rain and its making, the metal
of thunder, the split and steaming clouds.
I did not see before how well it fit me here,
how much I loved it: the weather slipping
me on like a costume, shrugging me off.

Despite Myself

In high school I wore
the standard uniform: sadness.
I remember the woods stretching
on and on, deer

walking the grounds like wise,
sensitive students. I remember
the gray light of a winter dawn,
my first love's arms—the body

with its hungers and vulnerability,
the clearing misted
with dragon's breath. That boy
played the same three records

over and over. I remember
his betrayals, the way I thought
his brilliance and beauty justified
any cruelty. I told him

I was afraid I'd die of wanting him,
and I remember the scent
of March rain on his wool jacket, the smoke
stubbed out at his foot. I remember

waking up, one night, from laughing
in my sleep, despite myself,

despite *the burden of terrible sorrow,*
as I took to calling it: what I thought

I would carry away
through those trees and bear forever.

Unreliable Clock

What if I opened you up, held
your wheels and hands, applied
balm or tinctures? You must be
a relation of mine—so maddening,
yet strangely loveable—and you make
a kind of sense to me. If I could see
your quirks and workings,
maybe I could even tell the time by you. Once
people lived without clocks; monks
told the length of an earthquake
by the number of *Ave Marias* said
during it. You are like that, only with you
it's hours that are disasters. You tick them
very slowly, trying to stay calm. Sometimes
they are so bad you tick them fast to be done
with them. Even the dog knows you're
unreliable (he's heard me cursing you, he
presses his nose hard against your face)—
but I could argue that you're lovely, and merely
unsettled—jumbled, like wind chimes: tolling
as best you can the complicated hours.

The Grassland

I keep returning
to where I am not remembered:

into the wind, among the long
cells of timothy and the thousand,

thousand grasses. The river doesn't
recall me, forgets my baptisms and slow

crossings against the hard current.
Sleep remembers me

no better, but convinces me
I can float from my skin

like a thought released.
Thoughts don't remember me—

they hang content as bats
under the eaves of the barn.

The bees keep no record of me,
nor do books—though from the time

I was small it comforted me to hold
my two hands in the shape of an opened book,

as if I could catch the world there
and read it from my own pages. The world

has no recollection of me—its indifference is plain
and holy. I've watched sorrow pass

through me and on like torrential rain;
I've seen the wind carry away smoke, and seeds,

and long strands of silver from my hair.

At the Window

From here, the slender birch
beside the pond looks like a young girl
in white, contemplating the water.
The morning sun, shadows

and silver across the surface seem
to be white swans, drifting.
Something about the angle and intensity
of light in this valley

makes them so convincing—every morning
I go to the window with my cup,
still groggy, believe my eyes before
I remember it's just the tree and light-sparkled

pond muck. And there's something of surrender
in that repeated mistake, the welcome play
of the senses before awareness—is it possible
I've been wrong about everything?

On the surface there still floats
an image at once beautiful and clear, as the tree
bends before the breeze, throws white-sleeved arms
out to the weightless and gleaming birds.

Describing the Bliss

It's not like peace, it's wilder, because my friend
had to take me in his arms and rock a long time
when he felt it, sounding some low, whole tone

in his throat, fully knowing we'd be sad again
and not caring; bliss is reckless that way. It's when
I dropped a whole handful of silverware

and the sharp spines of forks, knives clattered
with the simple significance of calcium—
silver minnows, their heads pointing in all directions.

It's the face of Christ on the back of a baking pan
and holy, holy, all my dreams have come true
and something low and large chimes around my ears

when I sleep. The living Buddhas of Tibet
are collecting white cloth for a flying machine
and the strange music of the stock market goes on

in its secret language. Our singular lives,
our singular deaths board the ark like animals,
two by two and we belong there—when we feel

the bliss it is because the world
has taken us inside its planed
and star-flanked hull, and we belong there.

www.ingramcontent.com/pod-product-compliance
Lightning Source LLC
Chambersburg PA
CBHW031301290426
44109CB00012B/678